WALKS FROM YOUR

Helmsle
the Hambleton Hills
by
Malcolm Boyes and Hazel Chester

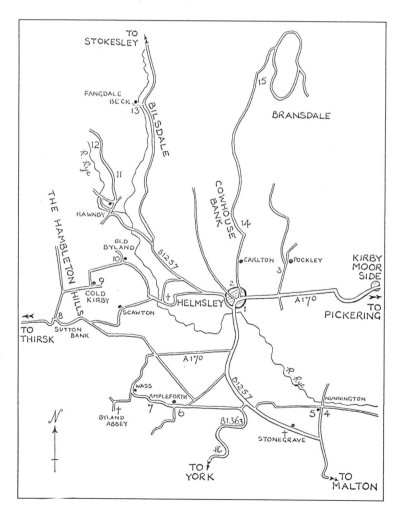

Dalesman

THE DALESMAN PUBLISHING COMPANY LTD,
Stable Courtyard, Broughton Hall,
Skipton, North Yorkshire BD23 3AE

First published 1993

Dedication: To Alan Chester.

ISBN: 1 85568 054 8

Cover map by Barbara Yates

Typeset by Lands Services, East Molesey, Surrey
Printed by Lavenham Press, Lavenham, Suffolk

Contents

Parking
EACH of the walks starts from a place where you can park your car, either in a village, in a car park or on a piece of land where cars park regularly. Please do not obstruct other traffic or farm gateways. A grid reference is given to pinpoint the start. Details for calculating a grid reference are given on Ordnance Survey maps.

Certificate
IF you complete all the walks in this book and you would like a certificate as a memento send an s.a.e. and 60p to 80 Howe Road, Norton, Malton, North Yorkshire, YO17 9BL.

Warning 1
THIEVES operate around the car parks in the area. Do not leave cameras, purses, handbags or other valuables on view in your car. Take them with you or lock them in the boot.

Warning 2
PLEASE drive carefully on unfenced moorland roads and give sheep and lambs the right of way.

INTRODUCTION

THE market town of Helmsley lies under the southern edge of the North York Moors National Park. The walks in this book take advantage of the rich variety of scenery in the surrounding area. It varies from the wild heather moorlands around Hawnby and Bransdale to the peaceful wooded valleys near Helmsley and Old Byland, from pleasant riverside walks at Nunnington to the wind-swept heights of the Hambleton Hills.

The walks vary between 3 and 6 miles. The longer walks are generally easier for route finding involves less climbing. The longest ascent on any walk in this book is on Wild Bransdale where there is a climb of 700 feet from Bransdale Mill onto Bilsdale East Moor, near Stump Cross but the whole walk is only 4¼ miles in length.

Equipment

ON a dry summer afternoon all the walks can be accomplished in sensible walking shoes. After rain some tracks may become muddy and boots may be preferred. You will require a windproof jacket as moorland breezes can soon make you cold and uncomfortable. With the uncertainties of the British weather it may be worth taking some waterproof clothing. You may wish to take a compass and the relevant Ordnance Survey map is Sheet 100 in the 1:50000 series. The area is also covered by the Ordnance Survey tourist map and in the 1:25000 series you need the North York Moors west sheet. You may also wish to take binoculars. a camera and nature field guides. The easiest way to carry everything is in a small rucksack.

Safety

IF you have an accident or meet someone else who has had an accident, render what first aid is possible – the local rescue team can be contacted by ringing the police. Don't let members of your group stray out of sight or get left behind. If the moor tops are covered in mist, or likely to become covered, in mist, choose a walk in the dale bottoms. The moorland walks with their extensive views are best attempted on clear days.

Problems with paths

THE walk descriptions are correct at the time of writing. Some paths may become overgrown in summer and some may be diverted but the new route will be well signposted. With modern farming methods, hedges or stiles may disappear or new buildings appear around farms, however the path should remain walkable. In case of difficulty, contact the Highways Department at County Hall, Northallerton.

Helmsley and the River Rye

Parking: (SE610838). Cleveland Way long stay car park, Helmsley.
There is a two hour limit on cars parked in Market Place.

HELMSLEY is set at the end of three different long distance walks. The Cleveland Way long distance footpath starts its 112 mile journey around the western and northern sides of the North York Moors National Park and then turns southwards along the coast to Filey Brigg. The 50 mile Missing Link connects the Cleveland Way from the coast near Burniston with Helmsley, offering the Cleveland Way walker a chance to return to his starting point. The 70 mile Ebor Way heads south from Helmsley to York then continues west to Ilkley. The second half of this walk is along the Ebor Way footpath to return to Helmsley.

This walk passes along the River Rye to a footbridge and the return is made along the opposite bank. You can include in the walk a visit to Helmsley Castle, still with its great defensive mounds and ditches and a number of buildings, despite being made untenable after a three month seige during the Civil War.

Also, you can extend the walk by 1½ miles and visit Duncombe Park (charge). The house was built in 1713 for Thomas Duncombe and now includes a 30 acre garden set among 300 acres of park-land. The house was badly damaged by fire in 1879 but has been rebuilt to the original design.

Start:
FROM the car park walk down Cleveland Way, cross the road and pass to the right of the church into the Market Place. Walk down Bridge Street, at the opposite end of the Market Place. Cross the bridge over the River Rye, taking care to avoid traffic as there is no footpath. Immediately after crossing the bridge turn left over a stile, bear right across the field and rejoin the river bank at a stile at the other side of the field. Turn right along the river bank and after 50 yards climb some steep steps with a hand-rail and continue through the woodland but take care as in summer this section can be a little overgrown. Below to your left is the River Rye. Eventually the path leads to a stile out of the wood and then, just over half a mile further on, the river sweeps left but the path continues straight ahead parallel with a fence on the right. This leads to a stile beside the river at the end of the field. Continue on the river bank to a stile then turn left over the footbridge.

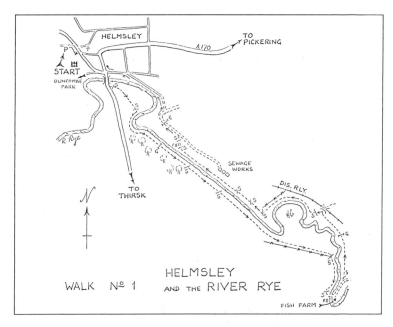

WALK N⁰ 1 HELMSLEY AND THE RIVER RYE

In front of you is a fish farm with different sized fish in the various oblong fish ponds. At feeding time the water appears to boil as fish swarm where food is thrown to them. After crossing the footbridge turn left and continue with the river on your left. Keep your eye on the river bank – you may see nesting sand martins in summer, their nests having being excavated into the river bank. When the broad track swings right carry straight on over a stile keeping the river on you left and a ditch on your right to reach a gate. Then continue ahead until you reach a cattle creep under the old Pickering to Helmsley railway line which was opened in 1874. The line continued south on this section to join the Malton to Gilling line. The line was closed to passengers in 1953 and finally closed to goods traffic in 1964 under the Beeching Plan.

Turn left at the cattle creep to a stile and return to the river bank, then follow a fence on you right to a stile beside the river where you turn right. This cuts off a large meander in the river. Continue beside the river and pass the sewage works. The right of way continues beyond the sewage works beside the river, crossing a small footbridge over a stream and then joins the access road to reach a gate. The road then swings right to a crossroad. Turn left, after 50 yards turn left again along the road into Helmsley. Turn left along Ryegate, then right along Bridge Street. If you wish to visit the castle or Duncombe Park take the first turn left. Return across the Market Place to the car park.

6

Ashdale and Beckdale

Parking: (SE610838). Cleveland Way long stay car park, Helmsley.
There is a two hour limit on cars parked in Market Place.

TO the north of Helmsley lie two wooded valleys, Beck Dale and
Ashdale. Although this is the longest walk in the book the route
finding is easy. It also gives the opportunity to identify a variety
of birds and wild flowers. In August there were brambles and wild
strawberries to sample and the flowers included eyebright, weld,
harebellls, purple vetch, lords and ladies with their orange berries,
meadow cranesbill, the ubiquitoius rosebay willow herb, self heal
and herb robert to name just a few.

After 2½ miles of walking up Beck Dale you climb out of the
valley and cross over the fields to descend into Ashdale for the
return to the outskirts of Helmsley. The route over the fields is
also used by walkers on the Teesside Hospice Coast to Coast walk.
A 154 mile walk which starts at Silverdale on the west coast, in
Morecambe Bay and finishes in Scarborough. The walk was set
up in 1991 with the intention of raising money for the Teesside
Hospice and can be undertaken as one continuous walk or over
a series of days or weekends.

Start:
FROM the car park walk down the Cleveland Way approach road
and turn left beside the main road. Continue on the footpath until
the road sweeps left and begins to climb out of the town. At this
point cross over the road and take the signposted footpath beside
the stream. Turn right over a footbridge and continue on the path
to a broad road. Bear left along the concrete road and fork to the
right at the sawmill. The broad track leads to a gate with a stile
on the right. Continue on the broad track along the valley bottom
with the wooded hillside gradually growing higher.

Threequarters of a mile beyond the sawmill, the track forks.
Bear right. Eventually, you reach a fenced off area where game
birds are bred. Turn right then left around the perimeter fence to
rejoin the broad track at the far side of the reserve. The wooded
heights are now closing in on you as the valley narrows. Cross a
narrow stream twice and when the stone track bears left and starts
to climb the hillside, carry straight on along a narrower path along
the dale bottom. After crossing a short boggy section the path
bears right and begins to climb up the valley side.

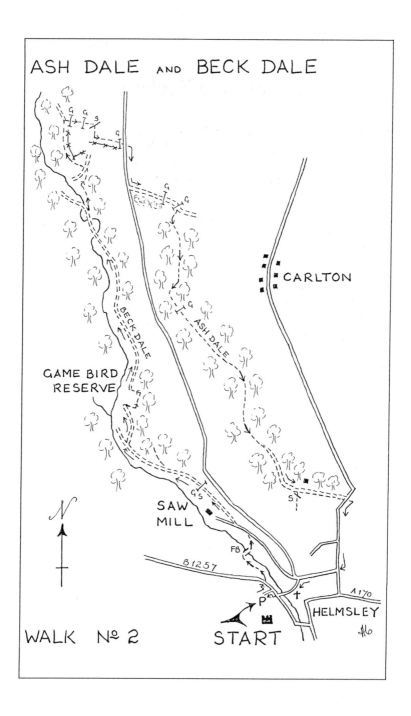

ASH DALE AND BECK DALE

CARLTON

BECK DALE

ASH DALE

GAME BIRD
RESERVE

N

SAW
MILL

FB

B1257

A170

HELMSLEY

WALK Nº 2

START

8

As you approach the top of the valley another track merges from the left. At this point you turn left on a path that passes through young trees and is parallel to fields over on your right. The woodland path then winds its way beneath more mature trees and although, in summer, bracken may be a problem the path should still be visible. When you reach a large grassy track turn right to a gate and follow the edge of the field with the fence on your left. Cross two fields and at the signpost beyond the stile turn right. There are extensive views to the south. At the end of the field turn left keeping the fence on your right till you reach a minor road.

Turn right down the road. At the end of the field on your left turn left at the public footpath sign and continue keeping the hedge on your right. The broad track passes through two gates and descends into a wooded valley. In the valley bottom turn right on a path that remains in the valley, do not follow the track up the other side. The track becomes clearer as you descend Ashdale. As the path continues beneath the wooded valley sides there is plenty of opportunity to identify a wide variety of flowers.

After two miles of easy walking the track leads to a road on the outskirts of Helmsley. Turn right and you can see the keep of Helmsley Castle in front of you. Take the second turn right, just beyond the Health Centre, along Carlton Lane. Follow the road when it sweeps left and pass the church on you left. At the main road turn right then left along Cleveland Way back to the car park.

Pockley and the Valley of Flowers

Parking: (SE635854). Take the Pickering road out of Helmsley and in 1½ miles turn left to Pockley. There is a broad grass verge on the left as you approach the village or you may be able to park in the village.

THE peaceful village of Pockley stands beside the road which leads up to Beadlam Rigg. Six of the houses in the village are thatched, The Moorings and West View are of cruck construction. Large curved pieces of timber were set in the walls in pairs and acted as roof supports. The old Forge was both a house and workshop for the village blacksmith and White Cottage is a good example of the old single storey long-house which contains four pairs of crucks. More information on cruck houses can be found in the reconstructed houses in the Ryedale Folk Museum at Hutton le Hole.

The walk descends into Riccaldale which in spring has a fine display of bluebells and primroses. In early summer you may also be able to identify germander speedwell, bugle, herb bennet, herb robert, lesser stitchwort, lady's bedstraw, meadow cranesbill, common sorrel, tormentil and silverweed. Also you will see as well as notice the smell of wild garlic.

Start:
FROM the parking area walk up the road towards Pockley and turn left before reaching the first farmhouse on the right side of the village. The broad track passes between hedges and swings left. When the lane ends, continue along the edge of the field keeping the hedge on your right. Enter the wood and continue to a gate, this leads to a track which descends into wooded Riccaldale. It is well worth keeping your eyes open for flowers and plants while you are in the valley.

At the bottom of the hill bear right then left to cross a foot-bridge. The river Riccal which flows beneath the bridge is often dry in summer but heavy rain on the moor can quickly fill the stream again. Follow the path up to a stoned track and turn right. Later, when another broad track merges from the left turn right along a narrower track downhill. This leads to a ford where you fork left keeping the stream on your right for thirty yards. Turn right over the footbridge which is a little difficult to see at first due to vegetation, so look carefully.

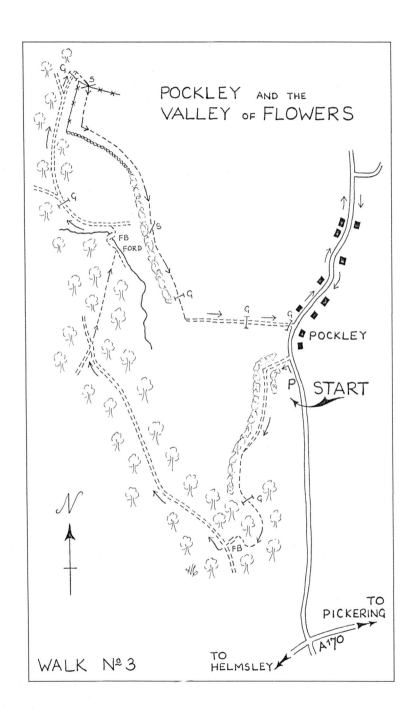

POCKLEY AND THE
VALLEY OF FLOWERS

FB
FORD

POCKLEY

P START

N

TO
PICKERING

TO
HELMSLEY

A170

WALK Nº 3

Turn left after crossing the footbridge then turn left on a track. Pass through a gate and fork right uphill on a broad track out of the valley. Fork right towards the top of the valley on a road which leads to a gate. Just beyond the gate turn right up the small valley side and turn right again to a stile over a wire fence. Follow the edge of the field above the wooded valley and at the end of the field turn left beside a broken-down stone wall. At the end of the second field continue with a hedge on your right. This leads to a broad track which turns left into Pockley.

At the road, turn left and walk through the quiet village to see the charming thatched cottages. In medieval times the village was divided into two manors, one owned by the Church of York and the other by the Helmsley lords. At the road junction turn around and return back through the village to the parked car.

Nunnington Hall and Caulkleys Lane

Parking: (SE668794). Take the Thirsk road out of Helmsley. After a mile turn left on the B1257 Malton road, after 3 miles turn left to Nunnington. Street parking in Nunnington.

ACCORDING to local legend, Nunnington Hall stands on the site of a nunnery suppressed at the beginning of the 13th century for immorality. The present hall dates back to the 16th century and contains a beautiful staircase and panelled rooms. It stands beside the River Rye and is in the care of the National Trust. Inside

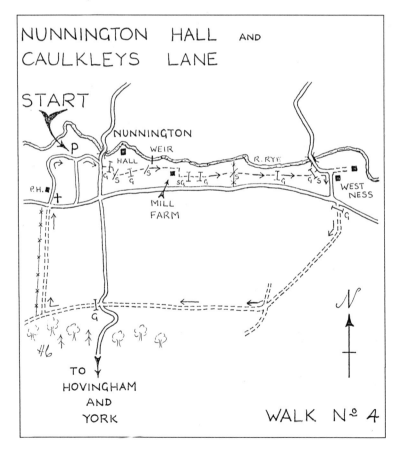

the hall is the Carlisle Collection of 22 miniature rooms, each reduced to one eighth normal size and decorated in different styles. Nunnington Hall is open on various days each week between Easter and October.

The walk follows part of the Caulkleys Lane, a ridge route along Caulkley Bank. There are fine panoramic views from the ridge and the lane provides an opportunity to identify numerous wild flowers and butterflies. On a summer day you may find field bindweed, field scabious, weld, lady's bedstraw, knapweed, meadow cranesbill, purple vetch, birdsfoot trefoil, harebells and both scentless and pineapple mayweed.

Start:
FROM the road bridge near Nunnington Hall walk up the road signposted Hovingham and York. After a hundred yards turn left at the public footpath sign, as you walk along the stoned track there are views of Nunnington Hall on your left. Pass through a gate and turn right on a grass path to a stile, then turn left beside a walled embankment and ditch; these garden features are called a haha. Continue straight across the field to a gate then cross the next field to a stile beside the river. At the other side of the stile is a seat overlooking a weir.

This was the point where water was taken off to power Nunnington Mill. Following the line of trees over the field you can see the mill leet which carried the water on your right. In 1890 the mill was operated by Christopher Foxton who was also a corn factor. The large building was probable used for storing corn as well as milling. Walk past the mill and immediately turn right; you can see the mill wheel still in position.

Continue for 25 yards then turn left to a gate and stile. Continue ahead along the edge of the field to a gate, then cross the next field. Two thirds of the way over the field the edge of the field bears to the left but the path carries straight on to a stile. Follow the line of trees to a hunting gate, then continue along the edge of the fields with the wooded banks of the River Rye on your left.

As you approach the road, bear left to a stile beside a gate, then turn right along the road through the hamlet of West Ness. Turn right at the junction. The broad grass verges beside the road lead up to a T junction, turn left for 15 yards, then turn right at the public bridleway sign stating "Caulkleys Lane". This beautiful green lane climbs steadily upwards, offering an improving view as you approach the top. In summer the lane has a wide variety of wild flowers to identify. Eventually the lane crosses a stoned track. Continue straight ahead and rejoin the lane at the other side.

As you walk along the ridge there are extensive views southwards to Hovingham and the wooded edges of the Howardian Hills, to the north across the valley of the River Rye are the North York Moors. When you reach the road, there are two seats on you right. Continue straight over the road where the track continues ahead. At the end of the first field on your right, turn right along a broad path with a fence on your left. The path descends to a road junction near Nunnington Church, the earliest parts of which date back to the 12th century. Continue straight ahead passing the Royal Oak Inn (or maybe stepping inside for refreshment) and other stone cottages in the village. At the bottom of the road turn right back along the road to the bridge.

Stonegrave Minster and a dragon's lair

Parking: (SE668794). Street parking in Nunnington. Approach as for Walk 4.

THE walk climbs steadily from the village of Nunnington onto Caulkleys Bank where there is an extensive view of the surrounding countryside. The gradual descent to Stonegrave is along a broad track that formed a 17th century race track for horses. It is still a bridleway to this day.

Stonegrave Minster contains a Celtic wheel cross, now preserved inside the church. The gritstone cross was discovered during restoration work in 1862. The minster, along with others at Kirkdale and Lastingham, near Kirbymoorside and Coxwold were possibly set up by St. Aidan. Aidan was originally a monk of Iona who became Bishop of Lindisfarne, off the Northumberland coast. He set up small monasteries around the countryside from which the monks could bring their teachings to the surrounding country folk.

The walk passes to the west of Loschy Wood which, according to folk lore, was the haunt of a dragon. After a number of knights had failed to rid the countryside of this evil creature, Peter Loschy took up the challenge with his dog. The knight joined in battle with the dragon but found that his sword cuts instantly healed on the creature, so severing of part of the creature's body he signalled his dog to carry the part away. As the fight raged the same tactics were used until the dragon was slain. In the hour of victory the faithful hound licked his master and passed on the poison from the dragon. So, although he killed the dragon, the knight died immediately afterwards. He lies buried in Nunnington Church.

Start:
FROM the road bridge over the River Rye turn right and walk along the road through Nunnington village, away from Nunnington Hall. Follow the road when it sweeps left and climb past the Royal Oak Inn to a road junction near the church. This is where Peter Loschy, dragon slayer, is buried. Walk up the track opposite, noting as you climb steadily the extensive view opening out behind you. At the top of the ridge there is an extensive panorama over the whole surrounding countryside.

Turn right on the broad, gradually descending track which was an old green lane used for horseracing in the 17th century. After

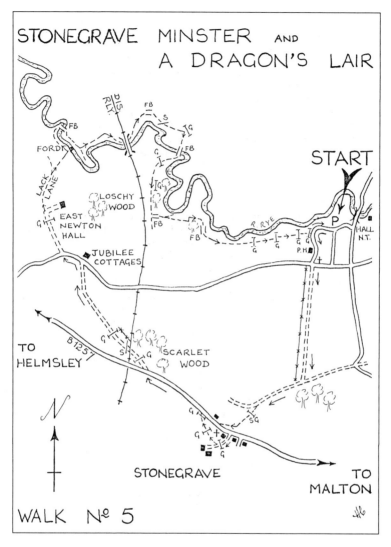

STONEGRAVE MINSTER AND A DRAGON'S LAIR

START

TO HELMSLEY

TO MALTON

STONEGRAVE

WALK № 5

nearly half a mile fork left down to a gate and cross over a stile. As you descend there is a view on the left over the village of Stonegrave to the wooded Howardian Hills. Continue down the old hollow way until you reach the road in Stonegrave. Cross over the road and turn left along the footpath and after 70 yards turn right along the road which leads to Stonegrave Minster. After visiting the church continue down the road to the farm, pass through a gate and follow the farm road to the right continuing in a sweep to a hunting gate in the field corner. Cross over the field to the top corner where a hunting gate lies behind a large tree.

Turn left beside the road for 400 yards on the wide verge but beware of traffic. Turn right and cross at the low point of the road and pass through a gate into Scarlet Wood. Follow the broad track through the wood, cross over the old railway line and descend the embankment to a stile into a field. Keep the fence on your right as you cross the field, pass through a gate and continue straight ahead along the track. Eventually it sweeps right to Jubilee Cottages beside the road and a plaque on the cottages tell you they were named in commemoration of Queen Victoria's Diamond Jubilee in 1897.

Turn left along the road and when the road sweeps left turn right at the public bridleway sign on the tarmac road to East Newton Hall. To the right behind East Newton Hall is Loschy Hill, the dragon's lair. When the road turns right to East Newton Hall carry straight on along Lack Lane. Eventually the track forks, bear right across the field to the River Rye, then turn left along the path beside the river bank. After 400 yards turn right over a footbridge and turn right along the fieldside path with the river on your right. There is some Himalayan Balsam growing close to the river bank on this section. Pass the ford where you joined the river earlier and after 200 yards fork left and continue on the river bank.

Pass under an old three arch railway bridge and at the end of the next field cross a small footbridge. Continue beside the river bank, then cross the next field to a gate where you turn right to a footbridge back over the river. Turn right to a gate and follow the track to the left. Keeping the fence on your left, pass a gate then turn left just before the end of the wood by crossing a sleeper footbridge over a ditch. Fork right in the wood. Pass through a nursery of young oaks then turn left and almost immediately turn right along the field edge with a wood on your right. At the river, turn right over a footbridge and follow bank path through several gates back into Nunnington. As you enter the village walk straight ahead back to the bridge near Nunnington Hall.

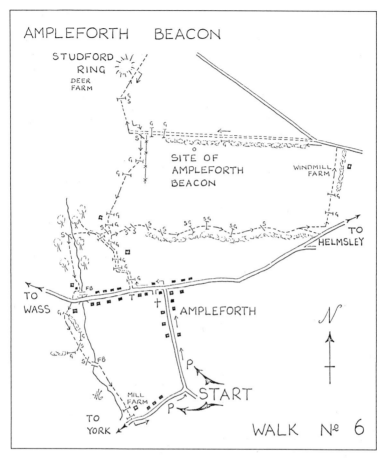

AMPLEFORTH BEACON

STUDFORD RING

DEER FARM

SITE OF AMPLEFORTH BEACON

WINDMILL FARM

TO HELMSLEY

TO WASS

AMPLEFORTH

FB

FB

MILL FARM

TO YORK

P

P

START

N

WALK Nº 6

Walk 6   **Distance 3½ miles**

Ampleforth Beacon

Parking: (SE584784). Street parking in Ampleforth, The top road through the village is used by cars and caravans diverted around Sutton Bank, so it may be better to park along the road to York.

THE walk climbs to the site of Ampleforth Beacon. Beacons were set on high ground during the Spanish Armada and threatened Napoleonic Invasion. There were three beacon sites around Scarborough, at the castle, on Olivers Mount and above Seamer.

19

Seamer Beacon would have been visible to Pickering Beacon. Ampleforth Beacon received its signal from Pickering and passed it on to Husthwaite Beacon, south of Coxwold, which was visible from Pen Hill above Wensleydale and York. On seeing the signal, local militia forces would have gathered at muster points. At these critical times the beacons were manned by two people during the day and three at night, with a sergeant who was responsible for ascertaining that the fire he saw was from a beacon and not another fire. To assist him during the time of the Napoleonic Invasion each beacon was issued with a telescope.

The speed which the signal could be passed was demonstrated in 1977. To celebrate the Queen's Silver Jubilee a series of beacons were lit starting from Windsor at 10.00 pm. At 10.20 pm the beacon at Sutton Bank, the ninth beacon in the chain, picked up the signal from The Chevin above Otley and Sutton Bank passed the signal on to Penhill above Wensleydale. I took only twenty minutes to cover a distance of about 200 miles.

The walk also visits Studford Ring, an earthwork enclosing an area of ground. On the inside of the mound is a ditch which is at the wrong side for use in defence. It has puzzled archaeologists so you can make your own guess as to why it was built. One possibility is that it was built to impound animals and the ditch was to prevent the animals jumping a pallisade fence.

Start:
WALK up the road from York and turn left at the top junction, then left again if you wish to visit the church. Continue on the road through the village and turn right up the signposted footpath opposite the telephone box. Pass through a gate beside a cattle grid and follow the tarmac road through parkland. Pass through two gates then turn right through a gate and climb to the top of the field. When the path narrows between two wooden fences turn right and keep the wooden fence on your left to reach two stiles.

Continue straight ahead keeping the hedge on your right. Eventually extensive views open out across Ampleforth to the wooded slopes of the Howardian Hills. Continue over the fields until you reach a long field. At the end of the field ignore a track which leads down to a quarry and the road. Continue ahead, turning left at the corner of the field. Climb to a gate then continue climbing beside a line of electric poles to another gate. At this point there is an extensive view over the countryside.

Pass through the gate and keep the hedge on your right until you pass over a fence to reach the road. Turn left and in 100 yards, when the road forks right, carry straight on along the green lane. This is a good area to look for wild flowers in summer. The lane gradually climbs to the high point which is where Ampleforth Beacon was situated. The view in the lane is restricted due to the high hedges but a look through a gateway to the left shows the view eastwards to Pickering and south-westward to Husthwaite.

Walk on along the lane, passing through two gates to reach a stile on the left. This is your way back to Ampleforth but first continue along the lane and turn right at the end of the field. Keep the hedge on your left to a stile beside a gate then turn right. Studford Ring is on your left with a deer park beyond.

Return to the stile you passed earlier and walk down the field with the fence on your left, enjoying the superb views. Pass through a gate and cross the next field bearing a little to the right to another gate. Continue keeping a wooden fence on your right, pass a wooden barn and you arrive back at the point above Ampleforth you passed earlier. Turn right over a stile and descend the slope, turn right for 20 yards on the track then turn left on a path which descends to a stream. Thirty yards beyond the stream, turn left over a stile into a wood and keep the stream on your left. On approaching the house, keep to the streamside and take the path beside the garage which leads to the road.

Turn right for ten yards then turn left; the public footpath sign is set at the opposite side of the road. Follow the track to a gate and stile on your right. Walk down the edge of the field, keeping the hedge on your left. Continue straight ahead between two gates to a stile then continue. Turn left over a stile and footbridge. Keeping the stream on your right, continue passing through two gates at Mill Farm to reach the road. Turn left beside the road, back to where you parked your car.

Byland Abbey and Wass

Parking: (SE573786). From the village of Ampleforth drive west on the road to Wass. After 600 yards there are two car parking areas to the left of the road.

THIS pleasant walk passes beneath the southern edge of the Hambleton Hills and, throughout the walk, the tree-clad hillsides are visible to the north. Approaching Byland Abbey, the Kilburn White Horse hill carving also comes into view at the same time as the abbey ruins. The walk passes through the small village of Wass which lies at the foot of the Hambleton Hills and the return is made along the edge of the hills with views to the south.

The only trouble Byland Abbey saw before its dissolution in 1540, was in 1322. Edward II had made a raid in Scotland in retaliation for a Scottish raid into Cumbria. When the English forces retreated back to Byland Abbey they were pursued by Scottish forces. The English forces were defending the high ground towards Kilburn White Horse but the Scottish forces outflanked the English troops and routed them. Edward II took flight to York, leaving Byland Abbey to defend itself against the raiding Scots.

Start:
FROM the car park walk down the hill in the direction of Wass. After 50 yards turn left at the public footpath sign over a stile. Walk down the field to a fence corner and continue bearing right to a stile. Continue straight ahead descending the field to a stile and footbridge. Bear right on the track over the field to a stile beside a gate.Bear left and climb up the hillside to a signpost where you bear right to a gate keeping the fence on your left. There is a pond and barn over to the right.

Continue over the next field keeping the hedge on your left. There are pleasant views on the right of the wooded slopes of the Hambleton Hills. Cross a stile beside a gate and carry straight on passing ivy covered Wass Grange over to the right. Turn left onto a track to a signpost. Continue straight ahead over the field forking right towards a gate then turn right beside the hedge to a blue gate and cross the stile.

Continue with the hedge on your left. The Kilburn White Horse comes into view and then the ruins of Byland Abbey. After 100 yards, turn left over a stile and continue walking with the hedge on your right for fifty yards. Bear left across the field at a signpost to a stile, then continue with the fence on your right.

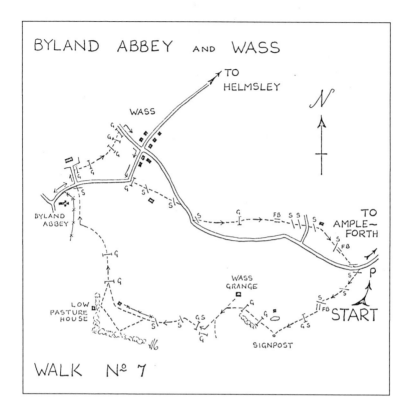

BYLAND ABBEY AND WASS

WALK Nº 7

The easiest way from here is to continue on the ridge to a ruined building, keeping the fence on your right, then turn right and descend to a gate. The farmer prefers people to use this route but the right of way goes a different way. It descends the hillside to the left down to the hedge and then turns right to a field corner. It then heads towards Low Pasture Farm but turns right around the garden hedge and crosses the field to the same gate mentioned in the preferred route.

Pass through the gate and cross the field to a gateway, bear left on an indistinct path until you reach the boundary fence of the ruins of Byland Abbey ahead. Turn right along the boundary fence and cross the field to reach a stile onto the road. The walk continues straight ahead up the access road to Abbey House but if you wish to visit Byland Abbey turn left to the entrance.

Retrace your steps from Byland Abbey and turn left along the access road to Abbey House. Turn right through a gate before the buildings and walk on to a gate at the end of the field. Bear left as you cross the next field to a gate in the top corner of the field. Bear left to a gate and continue walking to another gate which leads into a minor road, turn right down to the crossroads in Wass, the Wombwell Arms is set at the opposite side of the road. Turn right down the road through the village. It is worth examining the older stone cottages to see if there are indications of whether they were built with stones from Byland Abbey.

When the road turns right towards Byland Abbey turn left at the public footpath sign through the gate. After fifty yards turn left over a stile then bear right over the field, pass to the left of an electric pole and climb to a stile onto the road near the field corner. Turn right beside the road for 200 yards then turn left at the public footpath sign over a stile. Walk along the track over the field, pass through a gate and continue over the next field to a footbridge. Continue on the path to two stiles and cross an access road. Climb to a stile at the top of the field and pass a wooden shack on your left. Keep the fence on your left to reach a stile and footbridge, pass through some scrub and gorse to a stile which leads onto a road. Turn left up the hill back to the car park.

Sutton Bank and Hambleton Down

Parking: (SE515830). There are two large pay and display car parks near the information centre on the A170 8½ miles west of Helmsley.

THE view from Sutton Bank across the Vale of York to the Pennines is probably one of the most spectacular in Yorkshire. This walk starts off by visiting the view indicator to take in this magnificient panorama and returns back to the car park along the cliff top path. In between, the walk crosses Hambleton Down – one of the finest early racecourses in Britain which became nearly as popular as Newmarket. Its fine turf became the racing ground for the principal noblemen of the North.

The first races were in the early 17th century and Queen Anne, a century later, presented a gold cup prize in 1714. In 1719, the largest field of horses for one event up to that time took place when 31 runners competed for His Majesty's Gold Cup valued at 100 guineas, the race being won by the Duke of Rutland.

Many matches took place here, where, as the result of arguments, two horses were matched against each other for a wager. In 1799 a Mr Shaw won 202 guineas in a more unusual race. He bet that three of his horses could carry him 60 miles in three hours. By changing horses 28 times he won his bet with ten minutes to spare. He also won a second bet for five guineas that if he won the first bet he would die within three hours. He survived the gruelling experience to win the second bet.

The course declined in favour of York and Richmond, both of which could provide better entertainment for the gentry but still to this day horses are trained here.

The walk passes Dialstone Farm, at one time it was an inn which received some of its trade from passing drovers taking cattle to be sold in markets further south. The farm was near the finishing point of the racecourse and it was here that the jockeys were weighed in after the races. The walk then crosses the site of the former racecourse to reach the cliff top path back to the car park.

Start:
FROM the National Park information Centre, follow the signs for the White Horse Walk. Cross over the main road near the mile-

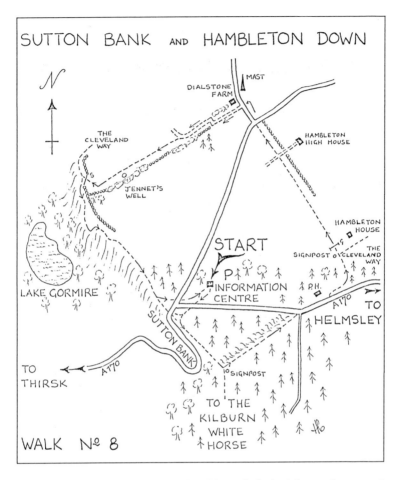

SUTTON BANK AND HAMBLETON DOWN

MAST
DIALSTONE FARM

THE CLEVELAND WAY

HAMBLETON HIGH HOUSE

JENNET'S WELL

HAMBLETON HOUSE

START

THE CLEVELAND WAY
SIGNPOST

P
INFORMATION CENTRE

P.H.

A170 TO HELMSLEY

LAKE GORMIRE

SUTTON BANK

TO THIRSK   A170

SIGNPOST

TO THE KILBURN WHITE HORSE

WALK No 8

stone indicating "Thirsk 6". After 20 yards fork right on the stoned path which leads to a view indicator and telescope. Take the path to the left which passes along the top of the cliff offering extensive views. After 200 yards look back and you can see Lake Gormire set below the cliffs and surrounded by trees.

After walking 500 yards from the view indicator, turn left at the Cleveland Way sign. The woodland path passes alongside Castern Dyke, a long embankment and ditch which may date back to pre-historic times and mark a boundary. The woodland path leads to a road junction. Continue straight ahead on the broad verge beside the main road, cross over the road and continue to the Hambleton Inn. Take the access road just beyond the inn which is parallel with and to the left of the road and is signposted "Cleveland Way".

The road swings left and passes through a wood. Approaching Hambleton House, fork left on a track signposted "Dialstone".

Pass through the gate, cross the horse walk and continue straight ahead. The radio mast on the skyline acts as a guide. Continue over Cold Kirby Moor keeping the fence and stone wall on you right. Eventually the track joins the road, continue straight ahead along the road for 100 yards then turn left in front of Dialstone Farm along the signposted public bridleway. You cross the former race course and at the end of the first field the track sweeps right, then left, and continues past High Quarry Plantation on a track signposted to Jennet Well.

Towards the end of the field you pass Jennet Well, a fenced-off well covered with a grill. Extensive views begin to open out to the north towards Boltby Forest. The path bears right alongside a wall to reach a stile. At this point you have a magnificent view westwards over the Vale of York to the distant Yorkshire Dales. Turn left on the cliff top path but keep control of children – don't let them stray too near the edge. As you walk back to the information centre you can look down on Lake Gormire set below you, eventually the view opens out towards Roulston Scar and Hood Hill to the right. Cross over the minor road and continue back over the car park to your starting point.

Cold Kirby and Scawton

Parking: (SE532845). Street parking in Cold Kirby. From Helmsley take the A170 Thirsk road and turn right at Sutton Bank to Cold Kirby.

THE walk starts in Cold Kirby and follows the Cleveland Way long distance footpath down into wooded Flassendale and Nettledale. A series of ponds can provide some interesting bird watching before climbing back onto the Hambleton Hills to visit Scawton. From Scawton you return to Cold Kirby through a wooded valley and over the hill top fields with some wide reaching views.

The small village of Scawton stands on the plateau formed by the Hambleton Hills and surrounded by wooded valleys. The church has served the needs of the local community since the 12th century and is clean and simple in appearance. There is a piscina, a stone basin for the water which was used to wash the sacred vessels. There is also a sedilia in the chancel, a seat cut in the wall for the priest. A pillared stone carving in the chancel may have come from the nearby abbey at either Rievaulx or Byland.

In the church entrance is a reminder of a local tragedy, a bronze plaque to the French crew of a Handley Page Halifax aircraft. They were killed when it crashed nearby on 15th March 1945 returning from an operational flight. Those who died were the pilot, navigator, bomb aimer, wireless operator and gunner.

Start:
THE village of Cold Kirby comprises a pleasant group of stone houses fronted by dry stone walls. Take the road which leads towards the church but before you reach the church, fork left at the wooden Cleveland Way sign on a path that descends into a small valley. Follow the path to the right, then climb to a wooden signpost where you turn left along a stoned track. This is Low Field Lane which offers an extensive view over the countryside.

Eventually the track leads to a gate and stile. Continue down the field, keeping the hedge on your right and this leads to a path into a wooded valley. At the bottom of the path turn left along the forestry track. At the junction of tracks in Nettledale turn right. After 400 yards, when the track sweeps right, turn left and in ten yards turn right to a gate and Cleveland Way sign. Cross the footbridge and continue to the stoned track.

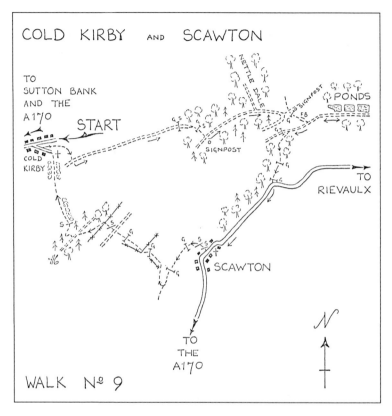

COLD KIRBY AND SCAWTON

TO
SUTTON BANK
AND THE
A170

START

COLD KIRBY

SIGNPOST

NETTLE DALE

SIGNPOST

PONDS

TO
RIEVAULX

SCAWTON

TO
THE
A170

WALK Nº 9

N

At this point, look towards the right to the gate and the grassy track which climbs away to its left. This is the track you will take to Scawton. First turn left along the stone track for 500 yards if you wish to see the ponds on the left for bird life. Return and take the grassy track which climbs to the left of the gate. This distinct path climbs beneath oak trees passing through two gates to reach a road. Continue straight ahead up the road into Scawton. The church is on your left.

In the village turn right over the stile near the telephone box. Cross a second stile into a field and after 20 yards turn left to a gate. Continue walking below the farm buildings until you join a track that leads to a gate. Follow the track into a small valley where you swing sharp right, keeping the wood on you right. When the track swings left carry straight ahead through a gateway and turn left keeping the fence on your left. Pass through a gate and cross a wooden fence and continue straight ahead keeping the wire fence on your left. There are extensive views to your right.

Pass through the gate at the end of the field and continue, cross over a broad stoned access road and cross the stile opposite. Walk straight over the field to a large tree and cross the fence just behind it. Turn left for 40 yards and follow the path as it bears right and begins to descend steeply into the tree-covered valley. When you reach the bottom of the dale turn left for 30 yards. Turn right up the indistinct path which almost immediately bears left beneath the trees then sweeps right and follows a distinct cleared line through the wood. Climb to the top of the valley, cross the stile into a field and continue ahead, keeping the hedge on your right. Cross the next field to a hedged lane and continue straight ahead, passing the church on you right, into Cold Kirby.

Old Byland and Rievaulx View

Parking: (SE550850). Roadside parking in Old Byland. Take the Stokesley road from Helmsley and after 1½ miles turn left, signposted Scawton. After crossing the bridge over the River Rye turn right to Old Byland.

THE village of Old Byland stands on the plateau of the Hambleton Hills surrounded by wooded valleys. The route chosen for this walk heads north-eastwards descending towards the River Rye. On the way you pass an excellent view down the valley of the River Rye to Rievaulx Abbey, 1½ miles away. The route then descends to a point near Tylas Farm. This was where the monks who founded Byland Abbey lived for a while. When the monks moved they retained the site as a grange and later it became a tilehouse, which was corruped to Tylas. The walk continues through woodland to Caydale Mill which was once worked by the monks.

The monks who founded Byland Abbey, which is visited in Walk 7, only settled on that site after a great deal of trouble and adventure. In 1134, 13 monks from Furness Abbey in Cumbria set out to establish another monastery in their area but four years later their church was ransacked by raiding Scots. Travelling eastwards into Yorkshire they were offered land at Hood, below Sutton Bank but this proved unsuitable for a large church. Next they settled near Old Byland but the sound of their bells clashed with the sound of the bells at nearby Rievaulx Abbey. The next move was to Oldstead, two miles to the west of the present site. Finally in 1177, after draining and clearing the area of trees they began building on the site of the present day ruins of Byland Abbey.

Tucked away behind the houses of Old Byland, just off the village green is All Saints church. It dates from 1145 but stands on the site of an earlier Saxon church, which may have been destroyed by William the Conqueror in 1069 during the Harrying of the North. Inside the church is a simple 12 century font and there is a Saxon font in the chancel. The exposed wooden beams of the 15th century roof can be seen. The porch through which the church is entered is also a bell tower. Incorporated in the porch are carved stones from the earlier Saxon church.

Start:
BEFORE you begin your walk it is well worth while to take a look at the little church. There is a signpost pointing the way over the

green. From the road junction at the top of the village take the road signposted Helmsley 5 miles. After 150 yards turn left just beyond the farm buildings over a ladder stile. Continue over the field to a gate then cross the next field keeping the hedge on your left. Turn right at the signpost along the edge of the field to a stile. Walk straight on, keeping the fence on your left and crossing several stiles until you join a broad track.

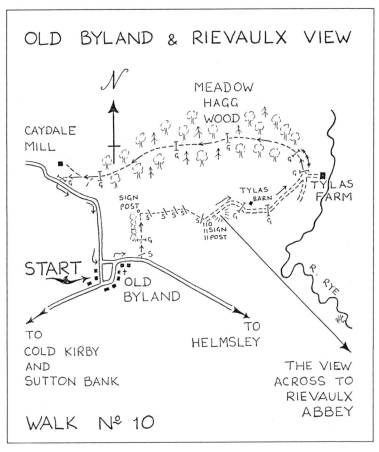

OLD BYLAND & RIEVAULX VIEW

WALK Nº 10

Carry straight on along the track with the valley of Oxendale on your right. After 200 yards the view opens out across Oxendale and down the valley of the River Rye to Rievaulx Abbey 1½ miles away. The extensive remains of the Cistercian abbey are clearly visible. Continue walking along the broad track and pass Tylas Barn. The broad track then begins to descend the ridge eventually arriving at a junction of tracks above Tylas Farm.

At this junction of tracks turn left through a gate with a sign stating "Keep dogs on a lead". Keep the fence on your right and the path leads to a gate into Birk Wood. The wood contains some conifers but the majority of wood is a mixture of deciduous trees so keep you eyes open for woodland birds. The bridleway is followed for just over a mile through the wood. Eventually you pass through a gate into a meadow where, in summer, there can be a rich variety of flowers beside the path.

After walking some 40 yards across the meadow fork right, then fork left at a bridleway sign and continue over the meadow to reach a gate above Caydale Mill which can be seen in the valley below. Turn left up the minor road which leads out of Caydale then turn right. A variety of flowers can still be found on these roadside verges. At the road junction continue straight ahead and turn left at the next junction back to your starting point in Old Byland.

Hawnby Hill

Parking: (SE539917). Take the B1257 Stokesley road from Helmsley and turn left to Hawnby. From the village follow the signs to Osmotherley. After 1¼ miles there is parking just beyond the cattle grid.

WHEN looking northwards from the Helmsley to Sutton Bank road or other places on the Hambleton Hills, two hills side by side stand out. Rising some 500 feet from the surrounding countryside Hawnby Hill and Easterside are prominent landmarks. This walk skirts the western edge of Hawnby Hill and then descends to the small church at Hawnby which nestles in the valley beside the river. After passing through Hawnby village the route follows the flank of Easterside completing a circuit of Hawnby Hill.

A notice in Hawnby church states that there are no priceless treasures but there is a wealth of history. It is old, having 12th century doorways, and was restored in the 14th century, possibly after being damaged by a raiding party of Scots but there is much of interest from the 20th century. A framed newspaper cutting hangs on the wall listing 55 men of the surrounding area who had given their lives in the First World War by the 23rd October 1916. There is a beautiful stained glass window showing a stretcher bearer carrying a casualty over the war-damaged terrain of northern France or Belgium. Another stained glass window commemorates the three sons of the rector of the church who were killed in 1917 and 1918. A third window is dedicated to 2nd Lt. Frederick William Orrey who died of his wounds near Ypres, in Belgium in 1917.

Start:
FROM the cattle grid take the signposted public bridleway which is on your right when facing Hawnby. Ignore the first fork on your left which is a path that is not a right of way, it heads towards the top of Hawnby Hill. Take the next fork left on the path which skirts around the edge of Hawnby Hill. On the way you pass the remains of two cairns. You can rebuild the pile of stones if you wish. You will come across these cairns all over the open moors, they act as guides to the paths. Eventually the path meets a wire boundary fence and then passes over a stile beside a gate. Continue with the fence on you left and as you approach Hill End House bear left around the buildings where the broad track continues to a gate.

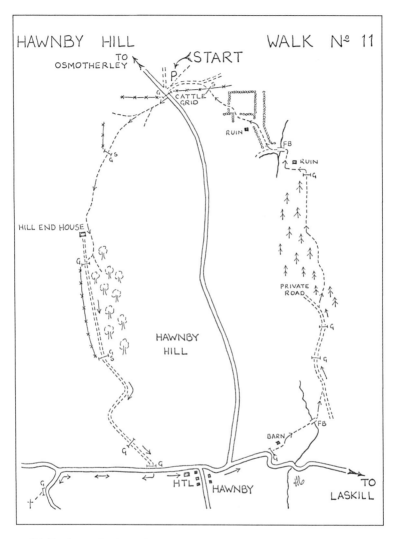

Walk through the edge of the wood and follow the track as it sweeps right, then left eventually passing through a gate onto the road. Turn right down the road and fork left to the church in its delightful setting beside the river Rye. Retrace your steps back up the road, passing the point where you joined it and continue into Hawnby village. The Hawnby Hotel is on the right.

Carry straight on at the first road junction along the Osmotherley road. Then turn right on the road to Laskill. As you descend there is an excellent view of Easterside Hill. When the road sweeps right, pass through a gate in front of you and bear left passing a ruined barn. An overgrown track leads down into a field which you cross to a footbridge over Ladhill Gill. Turn left after the bridge and continue until you merge with a stoned road. Walk along the gradually climbing access road for 300 yards, pass through two gates and fork right on an indicated footpath when you reach a private road sign.

The path climbs beneath the trees and then levels out towards the top edge of the wood. When you pass a clearing on you left you can see a fine view of Hawnby Hill. Eventually a gate gives access into a field, Bear left and descend some twenty yards below the ruined building before turning right on an indistinct path. Keep the stream on your left to a footbridge. Cross over and keep straight ahead for 100 yards along an old lane then fork right up a track which may be wet. Keep to the left hand side and when you see a ruined building in the field to your left bear left, above the ruin, to two gateways set in stone walls. Cross rough pasture to a stile onto a rough road then turn left back to the car park.

Hazel Head and Hawnby Moor

*Parking: (SE528929). From Helmsley take the Stokesley road
turning left to Hawnby. Take the Osmotherley road from Hawnby
for 2½ miles to Hazel Head car park.*

THE walk visits an old lime kiln and passes through woodland
before climbing onto the wide expanse of Hawnby Moor. There
are excellent views throughout the walk and the best time of the
year being August and September when the heather is in bloom.
The heather is a managed environment with section of the moor
being burnt off in rotation to allow young heather shoots to grow
for the young grouse. Some older dense heather is retained for
nesting and ground cover for the birds.

The lime kiln would have been used in the 19th century to
improve the acid moors by applying alkaline lime then ploughing
in to give better and more varied crops. Limestone would be
brought by horse and cart from the southern edges of the North
York Moors. The limestone was placed in the kiln separated by
layers of heather or moorland coal. This would be lit and the heat
would then crumble the limestone to powder which could then be
raked out at the bottom of the kiln. Further layers of limestone
and moorland coal could be added at the top while the kiln was
working until enough lime was obtained for the farmer's needs.

Start:
FROM the car park walk along the road towards Osmotherley.
The pleasant wooded section descends to a Z bend over Blow Gill.
Note the signed footpath on the right. Blow Gill merges nearby
with Wheat Beck and Locker Beck to form the River Rye. Set just
beyond Blow Gill is the stone lime kiln used for preparing lime for
spreading on the fields.

After looking at the lime kiln, return and cross over the footbridge over the gill. Turn left and climb on the path beneath the
trees until you join a broader track. Turn left and continue climbing
to reach a gate and stile. The path continues ahead passing through
the wood then bears left passing a ruined building on your right.
The path leads into a small field and then you bear left on a yellow
waymarked path that leads back into the wood. Continue with a
stone wall on your right until you reach a gate out of the wood
onto the heather and bracken-covered moors.

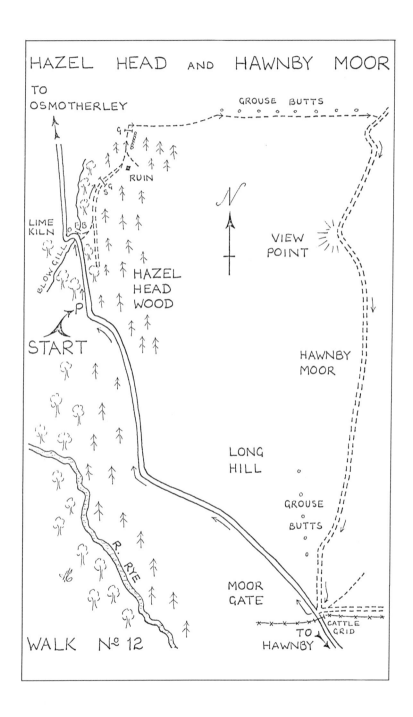

HAZEL HEAD AND HAWNBY MOOR

TO OSMOTHERLEY

GROUSE BUTTS

RUIN

LIME KILN

BLOW GILL

N

VIEW POINT

HAZEL HEAD WOOD

P

START

HAWNBY MOOR

LONG HILL

GROUSE

BUTTS

R. RYE

MOOR GATE

CATTLE GRID

TO HAWNBY

WALK Nº 12

Walk onto the moors for about 10 or 15 yards then turn right on a path that leads through the heather. You climb steadily keeping the edge of the wood on your right and a line of shooting butts on your left. behind you is Black Hambleton. The 1309 feet high hill is crossed by the ancient Hambleton Street trackway which may date back to prehistoric times and was regularly used as a drove road for cattle in the 18th and 19th centuries.

The path merges in with a track beside the shooting butts and continues to join a stony track over Hawnby Moor. Turn right along the broad track. As you walk down towards Moor Gate there are excellent views especially when the heather is in bloom, to the south are two hogsback hills of Easterside on the left and Hawnby Hill on the right. The path eventually joins the tarmac road at Moorgate which is the start for Walk No. 11. Here you turn right beside the unfenced moorland road then descend through Hazel Head Wood to the car park at Hazel Head.

The Heart of Bilsdale

Parking: (SE569946). There is limited parking in Fangdale Beck off the B1257 Stokesley road. There is additional parking for 2 or 3 cars at grid reference (SE574941) beside the B1257 where you can walk to Fangdale Beck. There is parking at the Sun Inn for visitors to the old cruck house, or the inn and if you start there begin at paragraph 3 of the walk description.

THE moorland valley of Bilsdale lies between Helmsley and Cleveland with the main road through the dale having to climb to over 800 feet at both its northern and southern ends. The only villages are Chop Gate (pronounced Chop Yat) and Seave Green at the northern end of the dale with the hamlets of Urra, further north, Fangdale Beck in the centre and Laskill to the south. The steep valley sides climb up to the heather moorlands.

The walk follows the western side of the dale from Fangdale Beck before crossing the river Seph to the Sun Inn. In front of the inn is a gravestone to Bobby Dowson who was buried in Chop Gate churchyard and had been whip to the Bilsdale hounds for sixty years. After his death a public subscription raised enough money to commission a gravestone. The vicar wouldn't allow the gravestone to be erected in the churchyard due to its design with foxes' heads and whips. The gravestone was finally moved to the Sun Inn where Bobby Dowson had cared for the hounds and spent many happy hours recalling both his foxhunting exploits and the cricket matches played on the nearby field.

Close by is the former Sun Inn built in 1606. The thatched cruck house has been restored by the National Park Committee and is currently open from 10.00 a.m. to 4.00 p.m. daily, except Thursdays, between Easter and the beginning of October. The building still contains two pair of crucks, curved timbers which meet at the top and form the sides and roof supports. The two inns have been run by the Ainsley family for over 200 years.

The return to Fangdale Beck can be made beside the road or an alternative route climbs then passes along the eastern side of the dale back to the hamlet beside the river. Fangdale Beck became noted in the second half of the 19th century for John Wood and his Bilsdale plough produced at his water-powered foundry.

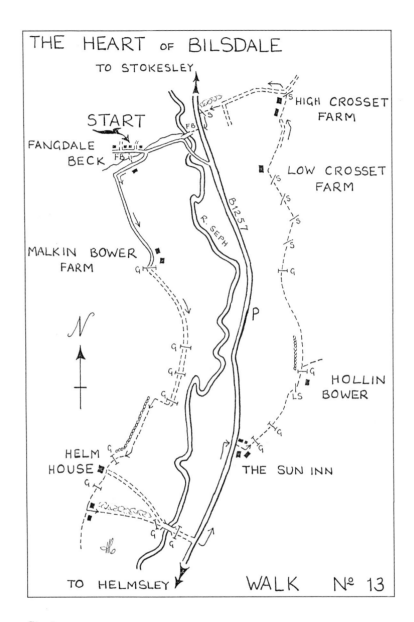

THE HEART of BILSDALE

TO STOKESLEY

START

FANGDALE BECK

HIGH CROSSET FARM

LOW CROSSET FARM

MALKIN BOWER FARM

R. SEPH

B1257

P

N

HOLLIN BOWER

HELM HOUSE

THE SUN INN

TO HELMSLEY

WALK N° 13

Start:

TAKE the right fork in the hamlet of Fangdale Beck and cross the white footbridge on the left over the stream. Turn right at the former chapel which is now a house along the road to Malkin

Bower Farm. At the farm pass through the waymarked wooden gate in front of you and walk along the broad track. There are some delightful views across the dale to the left. Pass through two gates and continue with the stream on your left. At the next gate, which is nearly opposite the Sun Inn, turn right up the field side, the route is waymarked. Turn left at the top of the field keeping a wall on your right.

Pass below the farm buildings at Helm House and continue to two barns on your left. Turn left between the barns and walk down the field with the hedge on your left to a gate. Continue straight ahead, crossing the bridge over the river Seph and up the access road to the main road through the dale. Turn left along the grass verge and turn right to the Sun Inn. The thatched cruck house which was the former inn is on your left. To complete the shorter walk you can return to Fangdale Beck along the road, turning left into the hamlet.

From the Sun Inn, take the path between the farm buildings which passes through four gates then bear left through a fifth gate and cross over a small field to a hunting gate. Cross over the fields to a ladder stile below Hollin Bower Farm. Turn left along the signposted path pass through a gate and carry straight on, ignoring the signposted path to the right. Keep the wall on your left and cross a short boggy section. Eventually you reach a gate. Continue over stiles across the fields keeping the stone wall or hedge on your right to pass above Low Crosset Farm.

Follow the waymarked path to High Crosset Farm which climbs to an old lane then descends to pass above the farm buildings. Turn left beyond the farm and walk down the access road. When it turns left, carry straight on over the field keeping the hedge on your right. Cross a stile and a set of steps descends to the road. Turn left and in 200 yards turn right at the public footpath sign down some steps and cross a footbridge. Continue straight ahead into the hamlet of Fangdale Beck.

Cow House Bank

Parking: (SE612886). From Helmsley take the Carlton road which turns left on the outskirts of the town. After 3 miles park in the car park on the left before the road descends Cow House Bank.

ALTHOUGH this is one of the longer walks in this book the route finding is easy. From the car park there is an extensive view northwards over the small fields and rough pasture to the heather moorlands beyond. The first part of the walk is along a forestry road, but the forestry is varied in size and not of regulation uniformity. At Roppa Edge you encounter a sculpture of an eight feet high irregular-shaped aluminium ring. It was one of two set upon the site, the other has been vandalised. The work was commissioned in 1975 by the Yorkshire Arts Association from Austin Wright, a sculptor who lived near York. Both the modern design of the sculpture and its siting caused controversy before it was erected on this plateau edge. The site forms an excellent viewpoint over the North York Moors. Part of the route back to the car concides with the Teesside Hospice Coast to Coast walk.

Start:
FROM the car park, walk over to the edge of the plateau and take in the extensive view northwards over Helmsley and Pockley Moors. The view to the right ends in the ridge of Birk Nab with Birk Nab Farm nestling on the hillside. Turn away from the cliff top and turn right along the broad forestry road. Pass over a stile beside the gate and continue along the broad track which gently rises for 1½ miles. Over to the right there are occasional views through the trees of Helmsley Moor extending to the horizon.

Eventually you pass through a barrier and continue over the moor to join a minor road near the aluminium sculpture. There is an extensive view northwards at this point. Turn left down the road which is gated at this point. On your left is Baxton's Wood and on the right is Helmsley Moor. The road continues down Baxton Rigg for 1½ miles and for half of this distance is unfenced with occasional trees to the left, the remains of a former plantation which may have been planted as a windbreak.

Turn left opposite High Baxton Farm along the signposted footpath. Pass through a gate and follow the broad farm track across the edge of the field and pass through another gate into a wood. The yellow sign of a man carrying a rucksack on the gate-

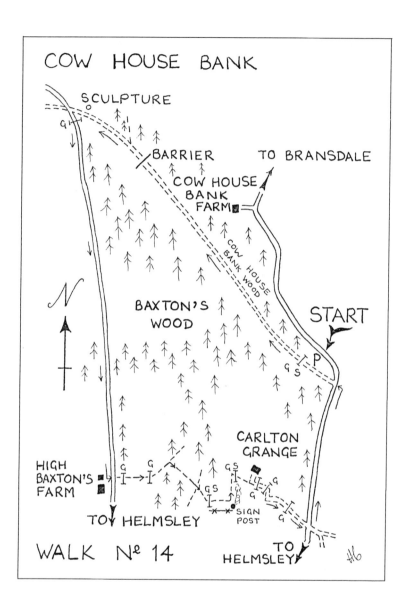

COW HOUSE BANK

SCULPTURE

BARRIER

TO BRANSDALE

COW HOUSE
BANK
FARM

COW HOUSE BANK WOOD

START

N

BAXTON'S
WOOD

P
GS

CARLTON
GRANGE

HIGH
BAXTON'S
FARM

G

G

GS

GS

G

G

G

SIGN
POST

TO HELMSLEY

WALK Nº 14

TO
HELMSLEY

44

post indicates the path is also used by walkers on the Teesside Hospice Coast to Coast Walk.

Follow the track in the wood to the left and after 70 yards fork right down a small valley. This descends to a point where tracks cross, take the one opposite which bears right up the wooded hillside. Cross over the stile beside the gate and keep the wire fence on your right. At the end of the field, turn left at the signpost and keep the hedge on your right until you reach a stile beside a gate. Turn right over the stile and along the track past Carlton Grange. Pass through a gate just beyond the farm and continue through gates along the farm access road until you reach the road. Turn left up the road for three quarters of a mile, then bear left back to the car park and picnic site.

Wild Bransdale

Parking: (SE609963). From Helmsley take the Carlton road which turns left on the outskirts of the town. After 8.3 miles park beside the road near the public footpath and public bridleway signs, before the road descends into Bransdale. There is futher roadside parking half a mile futher south.

BRANSDALE is the remotest of the inhabited dales on the North York Moors. Lying some ten miles north of Helmsley and Kirkbymoorside the approach from either place is over moorland roads which lead only into the valley. The greater part of Bransdale is owned by the National Trust. The small church in the dale gained burial rights in 1665 and the dead from Upper Farndale, to the east, were carried along the corpse road crossing over the moorland ridge for burial.

The walk descends to Hodge Beck which flows through the dale. It then follows the east bank of the stream to Bransdale Mill. This was a water-powered corn mill but there was also a blacksmith's forge on the site. The building was restored by the Vicar of Ingleby Greenhow, Rev. Strickland who had inscriptions carved on the east end of the mill house in Greek, Latin and Hebrew. The mill ceased working in 1917 but is now being restored again.

The long steep climb out of the dale begins by passing a sundial. It records the names of William Strickland, John Browne and Joseph Ward and the message "Time and life move swiftly". As the walk climbs above the farmland you pass through an area where jet was mined. The dealers would visit the dale and take the jet to the craftsmen in Whitby who would carve it into jewellery. On the moor top is Stump Cross set on the old road north from Helmsley to Stokesley and Guisborough.

Start:
WALK down the road and enjoy the fine views of Bransdale to the right. After 1000 yards, at the end of the wire fence, fork right at the public footpath sign. Descend, keeping the wire fence on your right. Pass through a gate and continue descending to a gate to the left of Cornfield House. Turn right for 15 yards then turn left through a gate at the side of the first farm building.

Continue down the field, keeping the broken down stone wall on your right, to a stile. Bear right and cross a small stream on a

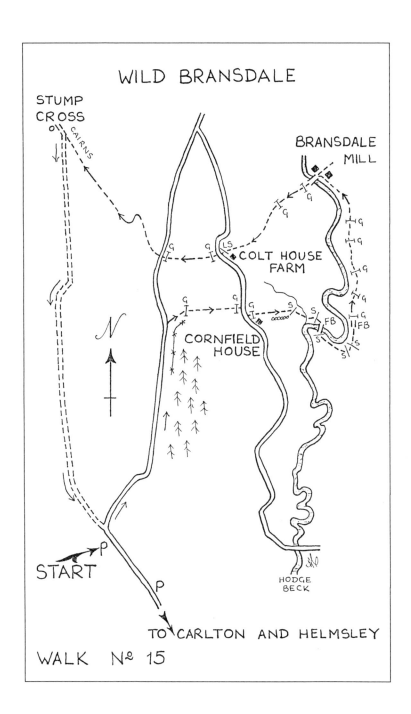

WILD BRANSDALE

STUMP CROSS

CAIRNS

BRANSDALE MILL

COLT HOUSE FARM

N

CORNFIELD HOUSE

HODGE BECK

START

P

P

TO CARLTON AND HELMSLEY

WALK Nº 15

47

single stepping stone. Follow the fence to a stone stile set in the wall. Continue beside the wire fence and cross a footbridge and stile, then turn left. Keep the fence on your left to the field corner where you cross two stiles and still keeping the fence on your left descend to a small stone footbridge. Pass through a gate, climb onto the edge of a grassy shelf and continue with the river on your left. A series of gates beside the river leads to Bransdale Mill.

At the mill, turn left over the bridge and carry straight on through a gate. As you begin to climb you pass the memorial sundial on your left. From this point there is a good view of the numerous buildings at Bransdale Mill. Walk up the track keeping the broken wall on your right, then continue straight ahead to a stone with a hole in the top and follow the paved track to a gate. Continue with a wall on your left to a gateway, then follow the edge of the field to a ladder stile beside a gate above Colt House Farm. Cross over the road and pass through the gate beside the public bridleway sign. The climb now becomes steeper and continues to the road above.

Take the track at the other side of the road indicated "Bridleway to Bilsdale". The path skirts what may have been a jet mine and continues climbing over the heather and through bilberry plants. Looking back, there are extensive views. Eventually the gradient eases and a cairned track leads over the moor to Stump Cross, the socket stone and broken shaft of a medieval wayside cross which stand beside a broad track. Turn left along this track back to where you parked your car.